CONTENTS

4

EARLY BIRD
ENERGY

MATTER

BY SALLY M. WALKER
PHOTOGRAPHS BY ANDY KING

LERNE⸏ ⸏APOLIS

Additional photographs are reproduced with permission from: © PhotoDisc Royalty Free by Getty Images, pp. 5, 6, 47; © EyeWire by Getty Images, p. 31; © Royalty-Free/CORBIS, p. 37; © Image Source Ltd., p. 42.

Text copyright © 2006 by Sally M. Walker
Photographs copyright © 2006 by Andy King, except as noted

Lerner Publications Company
A division of Lerner Publishing Group
241 First Avenue North
Minneapolis, MN 55401 U.S.A

Website address: www.lernerbooks.com

Library of Congress Cataloging-in-Publication Data

Walker, Sally M.
    Matter / by Sally M. Walker ; [photographs by Andy King].
      p.   cm. — (Early bird energy)
    Includes index.
    ISBN-13: 978–0–8225–5131–7
    ISBN-10: 0–8225–5131–4 (lib. bdg. : alk. paper)
    1. Matter—Properties—Juvenile literature. 2. Matter—Juvenile literature. I. King, Andy, ill.
II. Title. III. Series: Walker, Sally M. Early bird energy.
    QC173.36.W25 2006
    530—dc22   2005000583

Manufactured in the United States of America
1 2 3 4 5 6 – BP – 11 10 09 08 07 06

BE A WORD DETECTIVE

Can you find these words as you read about matter? Be a
detective and try to figure out what they mean. You can
turn to the glossary on page 46 for help.

atoms	ice	solids
boiling	liquids	states
cubic units	mass	steam
dense	matter	volume
evaporates	melts	water vapor
gases	molecules	

CHAPTER 1
WHAT IS MATTER?

Everything around you is made of matter.
Matter can be soft or hard. Matter can be any
color. It can even be invisible.

6

Matter takes up space. It can be weighed. Solid objects are made of matter. So are liquids like water and gases like air. Solids, liquids, and gases are the three states of matter.

All matter takes up space and can be weighed.

Matter has mass. Mass is the amount of matter an object is made of. A lot of mass is harder to lift than a small amount of mass. Prove it with an empty jug and water.

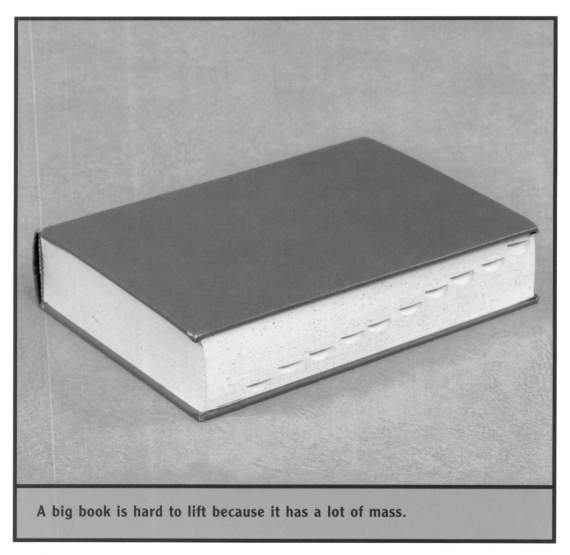

A big book is hard to lift because it has a lot of mass.

Air doesn't have much mass. A jug filled with air is easy to lift.

The jug looks empty. But it is filled with matter. Can you guess what the matter is? It's air. Air takes up space inside the jug. But the air doesn't have much mass. It's easy to lift the jug.

A jug filled with water is much harder to lift than a jug filled with air!

Fill the jug with water. The space inside the jug is the same as before. But it is much harder to lift the jug now. That's because the matter inside it has more mass. Water has much more mass than air.

Matter is made of tiny particles called atoms. Billions of atoms can fit on the period at the end of this sentence.

Atoms can join together to form groups called molecules (MAHL-uh-kyoolz). Molecules are bigger than atoms. But millions of molecules would still fit on a period.

Molecules are always moving. Some molecules have a lot of space around them. They can move freely. Other molecules are packed tightly together. They still move, but not as freely. Prove it with this experiment.

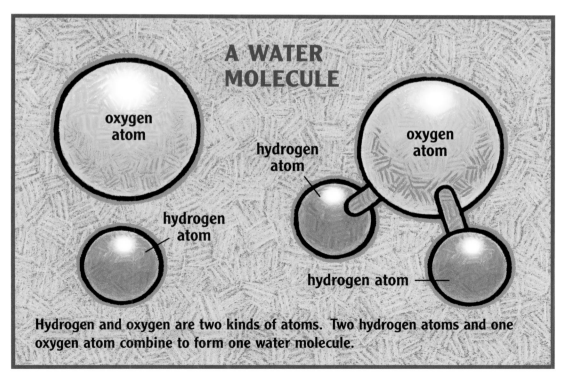

A WATER MOLECULE

oxygen atom

hydrogen atom

hydrogen atom

oxygen atom

hydrogen atom

Hydrogen and oxygen are two kinds of atoms. Two hydrogen atoms and one oxygen atom combine to form one water molecule.

Stand in a big room with two friends. Spread your arms like airplane wings. Pretend to fly around the room. You have plenty of space. It's easy to fly without bumping into your friends. Molecules with lots of space around them don't bump into each other very often.

These kids are pretending to be molecules that have a lot of space around them. They can move without bumping into each other.

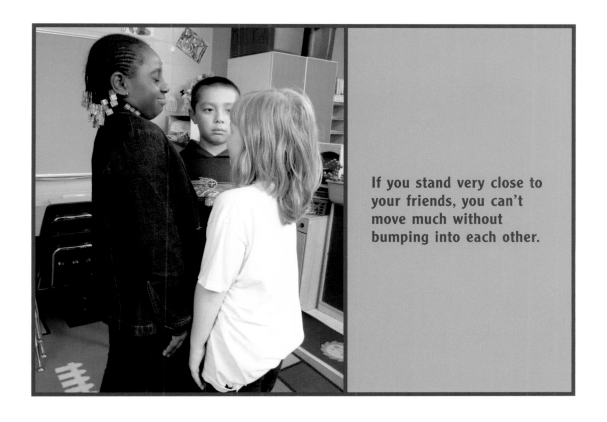

If you stand very close to your friends, you can't move much without bumping into each other.

Now put your arms at your sides. Stand as close to your friends as you can without touching. You are packed tightly together. You can't spread your arms without hitting each other. But you can still move. You can shake or jump up and down. When you all move at once, you may bump into each other. Tightly packed molecules move the same way.

CHAPTER 2
TAKING UP SPACE

All matter takes up space. The amount of space that an object fills is called its volume. To find the volume of an object, you must know its length, width, and height. The volume of a solid is measured in cubic (KYOO-bihk) units, such as cubic inches or cubic centimeters. A cubic unit includes length, width, and height.

Sugar cubes are solid matter. Each sugar cube's volume is about 1 cubic centimeter.

A solid object's volume always stays the same. You can move the object or break it into pieces. But it still takes up the same amount of space. You can prove this. You will need 27 cubes of sugar.

Put the cubes in a line on a table. Each cube is about 1 centimeter long. So the length of the sugar line is 27 centimeters. But this measurement doesn't tell you the sugar's volume. You need two more measurements. Can you guess what they are?

Make a long, narrow line out of the 27 sugar cubes.

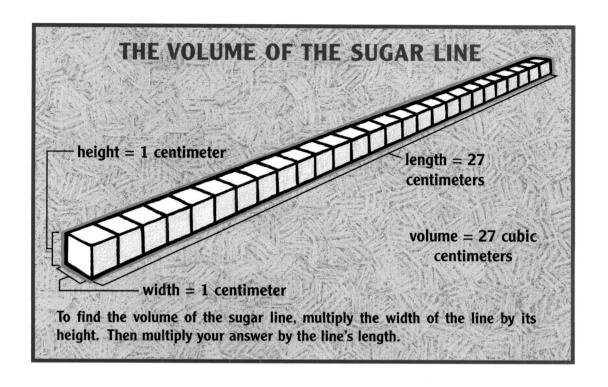

THE VOLUME OF THE SUGAR LINE

height = 1 centimeter

length = 27 centimeters

volume = 27 cubic centimeters

width = 1 centimeter

To find the volume of the sugar line, multiply the width of the line by its height. Then multiply your answer by the line's length.

To find the volume, you must also know the width and height of the sugar line. The width is 1 centimeter. The height is also 1 centimeter. Now you have all the measurements you need.

First, multiply the width of the line by its height. 1 x 1 = 1. Then multiply your answer by the line's length. 1 x 27 = 27. So the volume of the long, narrow line of sugar is 27 cubic centimeters.

Next, stack the sugar cubes. Put three cubes in each stack. You'll have nine stacks. Push the stacks together to make a giant sugar cube. The giant cube is 3 centimeters wide, 3 centimeters high, and 3 centimeters long. Does it take up the same amount of space as the long, narrow sugar line? Find the giant cube's volume and see.

Stack the 27 sugar cubes to make a giant cube. The cube will be 3 cubes wide, 3 cubes high, and 3 cubes long.

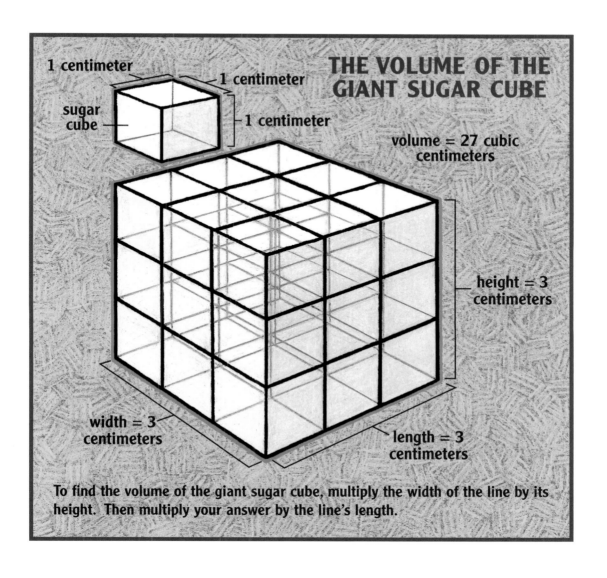

1 centimeter

1 centimeter

sugar cube

1 centimeter

THE VOLUME OF THE GIANT SUGAR CUBE

volume = 27 cubic centimeters

height = 3 centimeters

width = 3 centimeters

length = 3 centimeters

To find the volume of the giant sugar cube, multiply the width of the line by its height. Then multiply your answer by the line's length.

Multiply the width of the cube by its height. 3 x 3 = 9. Then multiply your answer by the cube's length. 9 x 3 = 27. The volume of the giant cube is 27 cubic centimeters.

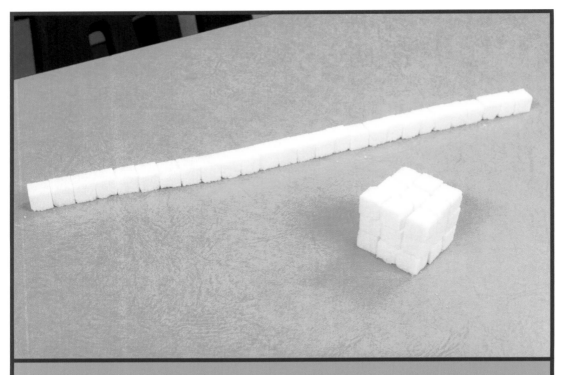

The giant sugar cube looks smaller than the long sugar line. But the giant cube and the line are both made of 27 sugar cubes. So the giant cube and the line have exactly the same volume.

The volume of the giant cube is exactly the same as the volume of the sugar line. The cube just looks smaller because the sugar blocks were moved around.

Chalk molecules are arranged in a certain pattern. If you break a piece of chalk, does the pattern change?

CHAPTER 3
SOLID MATTER

The shape and volume of solid matter always stay the same. Chalk is solid matter. Its molecules are arranged in a certain pattern. Chalk can be broken. But the molecules in each piece still have the same pattern.

21

These kids are pretending to be molecules that are packed together in solid matter.

Think about the moving molecule experiment you did. When were you more like something solid? Your group was more solid when you stood close together.

Stand close to your two friends again. Wrap your arms around each other. Now your group is really packed together. Its shape can't change. The molecules in solid matter always stay in the same place. The solid keeps its shape.

When the molecules in matter are very close together, scientists say the matter is dense. Molecules in most solids are tightly packed. So solids are dense matter.

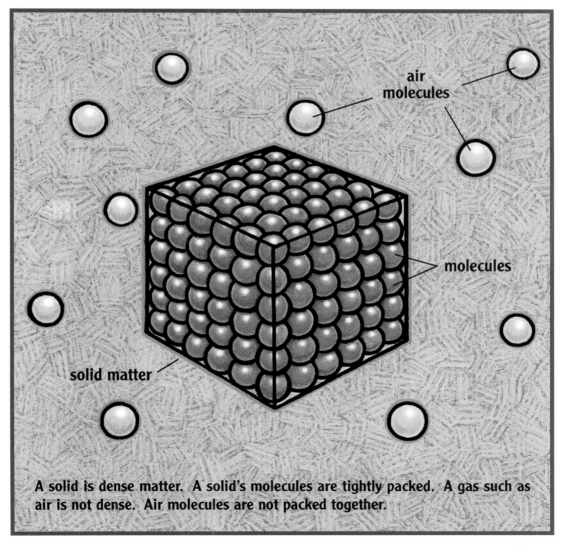

air molecules

molecules

solid matter

A solid is dense matter. A solid's molecules are tightly packed. A gas such as air is not dense. Air molecules are not packed together.

CHAPTER 4
LIQUID MATTER

Liquids are another state of matter. Liquids are usually measured in fluid ounces or milliliters. These units don't have "cubic" in their names. But they are still cubic units because they include length, width, and height.

Solid matter stays in hard chunks. But liquid matter flows smoothly.

The volume of a solid always stays the same. So does the volume of a liquid. But liquids are very different from solids. Fill a glass with water. Watch how the water comes out of the faucet. Does it fall out in hard chunks, like blocks from a box? No, water flows in a stream.

A liquid does not have just one shape. Pour the water from your glass into a bowl. See how the molecules quickly spread to fit the bowl's shape. A liquid flows into all parts of a container. It spreads out until its surface is smooth.

Liquid matter flows to fill the bottom of any container.

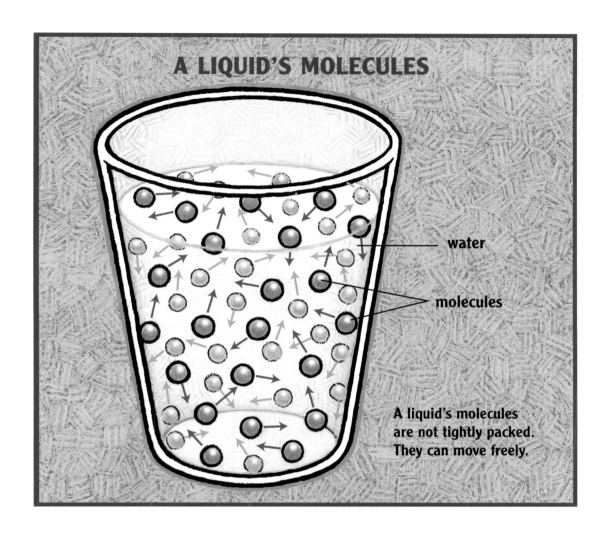

A LIQUID'S MOLECULES

water

molecules

A liquid's molecules are not tightly packed. They can move freely.

You can pour a liquid because its molecules can move freely. They don't cling together as tightly as the molecules in a solid. The liquid's molecules are not as tightly packed. Liquids are less dense than solids.

Some liquids are more dense than other liquids. You can prove it. You will need cooking oil, liquid soap, water, food coloring, a glass, and a measuring cup.

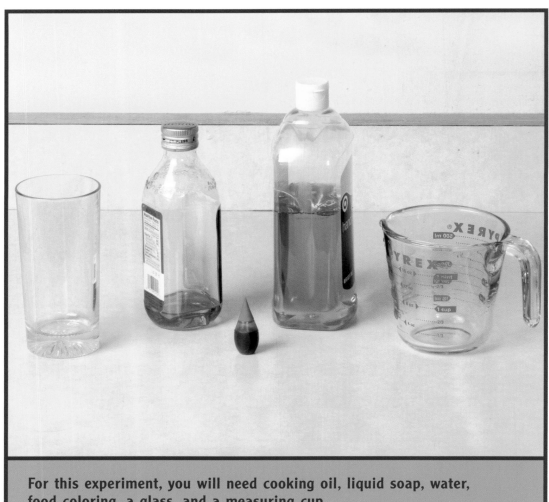

For this experiment, you will need cooking oil, liquid soap, water, food coloring, a glass, and a measuring cup.

When you pour the soap into the glass, it sinks to the bottom. The oil rises to the top. The soap sinks because it is denser than the oil.

Pour ¼ cup of oil into the glass. Now pour in ¼ cup of liquid soap. What happens to the soap? Why do you think it sinks to the bottom?

The molecules in the soap are more tightly packed than the molecules in the oil. Because the soap is more dense, it is heavier. It sinks beneath the oil.

Get ¼ cup of water. Add one drop of food coloring to it. Slowly add the colored water to the oil and soap in the glass. What happens? Is the water more dense than the oil? Is the water more dense than the soap?

The water sinks below the oil. But the water floats above the soap.

Air is a gas. Gases can't be seen. How can you tell when air is moving?

CHAPTER 5

MATTER AS GAS

Gases are the third state of matter. The molecules in gases are far apart. They are so far apart that we can't see them. But we know they are there. We can't see air. But we can see leaves blow in the wind. Wind is moving air.

Gases are invisible. But they still take up space, just like solids and liquids. You can prove this with a drinking straw and a tiny piece of paper.

A straw looks empty. But it is filled with air.

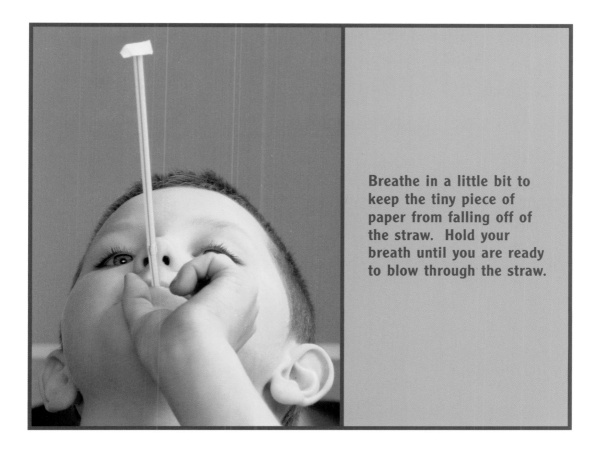

Breathe in a little bit to keep the tiny piece of paper from falling off of the straw. Hold your breath until you are ready to blow through the straw.

Look at the straw. Is it filled with anything? Yes, it's filled with air. Put one end of the straw in your mouth. Look up at the ceiling. Balance the tiny paper on the other end of the straw. Now blow through the straw.

What happens to the paper? It blows off. Why does this happen?

The air leaving your mouth needs space. It pushes the air that is already in the straw. The straw's air pushes against the paper. It pushes the paper away.

When you blow air through the straw, the air pushes the paper off of the straw.

When you blow air bubbles in water, the air moves up and out of the water.

Like liquids, gases can change shape. The molecules in gases move around even more freely than the molecules in liquids. If you blow air into a glass, the air does not stay at the bottom. Instead, air molecules flow freely up and out of the glass.

To keep a gas in a container, you must completely enclose it. Blow air into a balloon. If you don't hold the balloon closed, the air rushes out. But if you tie the balloon, the gas is enclosed. The balloon stays full.

A gas spreads out to fill whatever container it is in. The air from your small balloon could spread out to fill a whole room.

To keep air in a balloon, you have to hold the balloon closed or tie its neck. Otherwise, the air rushes out.

When ice melts, it changes from the solid state to the liquid state. What makes molecules change from one state to another?

CHAPTER 6

MATTER CAN CHANGE STATE

Matter can change from one state to another. Adding heat to matter makes molecules move faster. Taking away heat makes them move slower. When molecules move faster or slower, they can change state.

You know water in all three states. Solid water is called ice. When ice melts, it turns into liquid water. When liquid water evaporates (ee-VAP-uhr-ayts), it changes into a gas.

You can make water change its state. You will need a pot holder, a small pan, a stove or hot plate, and a few ice cubes. Wear safety glasses, and ask an adult to help you.

To make water change its state, you need a pan, a stove or hot plate, safety glasses, and some ice cubes.

Put a few ice cubes into the pan. Then turn on the burner.

Dump the ice cubes into the pan. Put the pan on the stove or hot plate. Turn the burner on. What happens to the ice cubes as they are heated? They melt. The solid ice changes into liquid water.

As the water heats, can you see bubbles? What do you think is inside the bubbles? Water vapor is inside them. Water vapor is water in the gas state.

Heat from the burner makes the solid ice cubes melt. They become liquid water.

The bubbles in boiling water are made of water vapor. The bubbles rise to the surface and pop. Then the water vapor goes up into the air.

How do the bubbles move as the water gets hotter? They rise to the top. Soon the water's surface will be bubbling fast. This is called boiling. The gas bubbles pop and escape from the pan. They form a cloud of steam. Steam is hot water vapor.

You have made matter change its state. Your solid ice cubes changed into liquid water. Then the liquid changed into a gas.

Our world is made of matter. Everything around you is a solid, a liquid, or a gas. Your lunch is made of matter. What kind of matter did you eat today?

An apple is solid matter.

You take up space and you can be weighed. So you are made of matter.

Even you are made of matter. Can you name any of the solids, liquids, and gases in your body? It's a question that really matters!

ON SHARING A BOOK

When you share a book with a child, you show that reading is important. To get the most out of the experience, read in a comfortable, quiet place. Turn off the television and limit other distractions, such as telephone calls. Be prepared to start slowly. Take turns reading parts of this book. Stop occasionally and discuss what you're reading. Talk about the photographs. If the child begins to lose interest, stop reading. When you pick up the book again, revisit the parts you have already read.

BE A VOCABULARY DETECTIVE

The word list on page 5 contains words that are important in understanding the topic of this book. Be word detectives and search for the words as you read the book together. Talk about what the words mean and how they are used in the sentence. Do any of these words have more than one meaning? You will find the words defined in a glossary on page 46.

WHAT ABOUT QUESTIONS?

Use questions to make sure the child understands the information in this book. Here are some suggestions:

> What did this paragraph tell us? What does this picture show? What do you think we'll learn about next? What are the three states of matter? Which is denser, a solid or a gas? Why can you pour a liquid but not a solid? What is solid water called? What is your favorite part of the book? Why?

If the child has questions, don't hesitate to respond with questions of your own, such as: What do *you* think? Why? What is it that you don't know? If the child can't remember certain facts, turn to the index.

INTRODUCING THE INDEX

The index helps readers find information without searching through the whole book. Turn to the index on page 48. Choose an entry such as *atoms* and ask the child to use the index to find out what a group of atoms is called. Repeat with as many entries as you like. Ask the child to point out the differences between an index and a glossary. (The index helps readers find information, while the glossary tells readers what words mean.)

LEARN MORE ABOUT MATTER

BOOKS

Angliss, Sarah. *Matter and Materials.* New York: Kingfisher, 2001. This book has lots of experiments about the states of matter and more.

Ballard, Carol. *Solids, Liquids, and Gases: From Ice Cubes to Bubbles.* Chicago: Heinemann Library, 2004. Find out about solids, liquids, and gases through experiments that you can do at home.

Cobb, Vicki. *Why Can't You Unscramble an Egg?: And Other Not So Dumb Questions about Matter.* New York: Lodestar Books, 1990. Find out how much air weighs, why an ice cube floats, and more.

Darling, David J. *From Glasses to Gases: The Science of Matter.* New York: Dillon, 1992. Find out why ketchup sticks in the bottle until you shake it, how soapy water washes away grease, and more. Many experiments are included.

Tocci, Salvatore. *Experiments with Solids, Liquids, and Gases.* New York: Children's Press, 2001. This book is packed with experiments about matter.

WEBSITES

Water
http://www.nyu.edu/pages/mathmol/textbook/3gradecover.html
Find out all about water as a solid, a liquid, and a gas. Activities are included.

States of Matter
http://www.harcourtschool.com/activity/states_of_matter/index.html
Click on gas, liquid, or solid to get a close-up view of how molecules move.

Materials: Solids, Liquids, and Gases
http://www.bbc.co.uk/schools/revisewise/science/materials/08_act.shtml
This site has information about the states of matter, plus activities and quizzes.

GLOSSARY

atoms: the tiny particles that make up all things

boiling: bubbling and changing from a liquid into a gas

cubic (KYOO-bihk) units: units for measuring the amount of space things fill

dense: having molecules that are very close together

evaporates (ee-VAP-uhr-ayts): changes from a liquid into a gas

gases: substances that can change their size and their shape. A gas can spread out to fill any container.

ice: solid water

liquids: substances that flow easily. A liquid always stays the same size, but its shape can change.

mass: the amount of matter an object is made of

matter: what all things are made of. Matter takes up space and can be weighed.

melts: changes from a solid into a liquid

molecules (MAHL-uh-kyoolz): the smallest pieces that a substance can be broken into. A molecule is made up of atoms that are joined together.

solids: substances that stay the same size and the same shape. The molecules in most solids are tightly packed.

states: the solid, liquid, and gas forms of matter

steam: water in the gas state

volume: the amount of space that an object fills

water vapor: water in the gas state

INDEX

Pages listed in **bold** type refer to photographs.